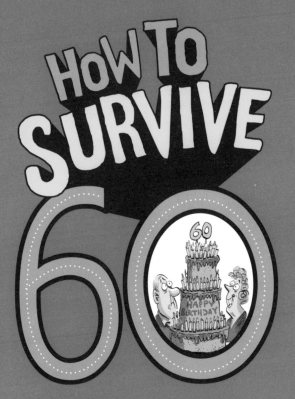

HOW TO SURVIVE 60

MIKE HASKINS AND CLIVE WHICHELOW
ILLUSTRATIONS BY IAN BAKER

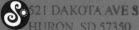

summersdale

HOW TO SURVIVE 60

Summersdale Publishers Ltd
46 West Street
Chichester
West Sussex
PO19 1RP
UK

www.summersdale.com

Printed and bound in China

ISBN: 978-1-84953-937-1

Substantial discounts on bulk quantities of Summersdale books are available to corporations, professional associations and other organisations. For details contact Nicky Douglas by telephone: +44 (0) 1243 756902, fax: +44 (0) 1243 786300 or email: nicky@summersdale.com.

To.................................

From.............................

INTRODUCTION

Let's be honest – it will take a bit of getting used to, this hitting 60 lark. Once you'd got over the shock of hitting 50, then 51 didn't sound very much worse. Or 52 or 53…

But those innocuous-sounding little ages just quietly slipped by until, shock horror, you were 59. You tried to make it last. You eked it out; 59 was a lovely long last year of being in your fifties. Sounds so young now, doesn't it?

See, there's the trick. And it will be the same with 60. At some point you will look back and think, 'Ah, sixty, that wasn't old at all was it?' Well, think it now and that's the first step in surviving! Don't worry, it's all going to be lovely.

TYPES OF 60-YEAR-OLD YOU COULD BE

The 'I Can't Believe He/She is 60' year old, who looks 20 years younger simply because they have stayed relatively slim and still have a reasonable covering of hair on their head (which has mysteriously not gone grey)

. . . .

The 'I'm Now an Old Fogey and I'm Going to Exploit It For All It's Worth' type, who now moans about everything and demands discounts everywhere

. . . .

The marathon-running, onesie-wearing, Facebook-using dude, who is really a born-again teenager but without the attitude

HOW TO SURVIVE

The all-natural 60-year-old,
who lets everything grow
and hang out and who might
be mistaken for the wild
man or woman of the woods

REALISTIC AND UNREALISTIC GOALS IN YOUR NEW LIFE AS A 60-YEAR-OLD

REALISTIC GOAL	UNREALISTIC GOAL
To fan the flames of passion now and again	To find old flames are passionate about you once again
To keep your weight down by being sensible	To hold weights up by being a bodybuilder
To put something back into your local community by becoming a local councillor	To clean up your local community by becoming a superhero
To write your autobiography as a memento for your grandchildren	To write your autobiography as a vehicle for a major Hollywood star

GADGETS A 60-YEAR-OLD MIGHT NEED

A walking stick with a built-in electric stunner to help you clear a path through a crowded street

. . . .

Glow-in-the-dark pyjamas to stop you bumping into things on those early-hours trips to the toilet

. . . .

Taste bud implants to help you regain your youthful enjoyment of food

A device that will provide
instant subtitles when
you are attempting
to communicate with
mumbling youngsters

FINANCIAL OUTGOINGS FROM NOW ON (60-YEAR-OLD MEN)

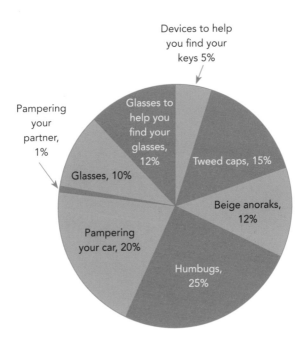

Devices to help you find your keys 5%

Pampering your partner, 1%

Glasses to help you find your glasses, 12%

Glasses, 10%

Tweed caps, 15%

Beige anoraks, 12%

Pampering your car, 20%

Humbugs, 25%

HOW TO AVOID BEING 60 EVEN WHEN YOU ARE IN YOUR SIXTIES

Get a job as an action movie stunt performer – what could possibly go wrong?

. . . .

Refuse to respond to salutations such as 'Hey gramps' or jocular supermarket cashiers who ask if you're over 18 when buying alcohol

. . . .

Insist on paying for your bus journeys – though the words 'nose' 'spite' and 'face' come to mind

Become a nightclub DJ –
albeit one who exclusively
plays records from several
decades ago and all at
an agreeable volume

WHY 60 IS DIFFERENT FROM 50

There is a great wisdom that you achieve at 60. If only you could remember what it was…

. . . .

You will find that the average speed at which you move has become inversely proportional to your age

. . . .

You may find that your waist measurement is doing its utmost to keep up with your age too

. . . .

At 60, you are entitled to free stuff such as bus travel and medical prescriptions – time to fill your boots!

CLOTHES YOU PROBABLY SHOULDN'T BE WEARING NOW (MEN)

The football kit of your local non-league team – no matter how badly they're doing, it is now very unlikely you will be invited on to the pitch if they find themselves a man down

. . . .

A branded baseball cap – although it will keep people wondering if you have any hair underneath it

. . . .

A traffic cone – and being drunk is no excuse

HOW TO SURVIVE

Large amounts of chunky
jewellery – if nothing else,
the weight will make it
even more difficult for you
to get up from your chair

CHANGES THAT MAY OCCUR IN YOUR APPEARANCE DURING YOUR SIXTIES

NORMAL	NOT SO NORMAL
Grey hair	Matching grey skin
Glasses on a string around your neck	Your name and address on a string around your neck
Your teeth look whiter and straighter than they ever did before	Your new teeth only chew food if you wind them up first
Your face looks lined and lived in	The lines on your face turn out to be literally lived in by species previously unknown to man

CLOTHES YOU PROBABLY SHOULDN'T BE WEARING NOW (WOMEN)

Anything with 'mini' or 'micro' in its name

. . . .

Anything see-through – apart
from your bifocals, of course

. . . .

A T-shirt with a picture of a boy band
on it – even if it is The Osmonds

HOW TO SURVIVE

Shoes with heels so
high you need a stairlift
to get into them

PEOPLE IT WILL BE INAPPROPRIATE FOR YOU TO HANG OUT WITH

People who fail to understand
your references to TV shows that
were broadcast 50 years ago

. . . .

Those who like to hit the town at the
time that you usually like to hit the sack

. . . .

People who are speaking a
version of English that you cannot
comprehend – soz, whatevs, lol

PEOPLE WHOSE USUAL MEETING PLACE IS THE BACK OF THE BIKE SHED

FINANCIAL OUTGOINGS FROM NOW ON (60-YEAR-OLD WOMEN)

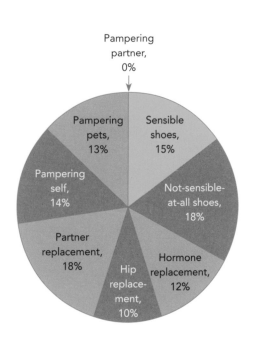

Pampering partner, 0%

Pampering pets, 13%

Sensible shoes, 15%

Pampering self, 14%

Not-sensible-at-all shoes, 18%

Partner replacement, 18%

Hip replacement, 10%

Hormone replacement, 12%

WAYS TO DEFY AGEING WITHOUT RESORTING TO COSMETIC SURGERY

Start drinking alcopops

. . . .

Include the word 'like' in all
of your sentences

. . . .

On a night out, say your parents will
be wondering where you are

Learn to text with one
hand – your grandkids
will be stunned!

ACTIVITIES THAT WILL NOW CAUSE YOU TO PUT YOUR BACK OUT

Scratching your back

. . . .

Indicating where your back needs scratching to your partner who is annoyingly reluctant to scratch it for you

. . . .

Trying to treat a spot that has developed in an inconvenient location on your back

. . . .

Simultaneously trying to see and cut your toenails

LIFESTYLE CHANGES

You will become increasingly reluctant
to replace your old technological
devices (which seem to go out
of date faster and faster)

. . . .

You start turning the sound up on
your TV and telling young people
to turn their music down

. . . .

When clothes shopping your main
question will be 'Is this comfy?'
rather than 'Is this trendy?'

It is now obligatory for you to carry a tin of boiled sweets on the dashboard of your car at all times

A GUIDE TO THE ITEMS THAT A 60-YEAR-OLD MAY KEEP IN THE CUPBOARD

ILL-ADVISED	SENSIBLE	OVERCAUTIOUS
A pair of speed skates for going out in icy conditions	Warm winter clothes and a pair of wellies	A team of brandy-bearing huskies and a Sherpa
A book entitled *The Absolute Idiot's Guide to Plumbing*	The business cards of some reasonably priced emergency plumbers	A tunnel down to a natural spring in case your water's cut off
A book entitled *The Absolute Idiot's Guide to Rewiring Your House*	Candles in case of a power cut	An electric generator that can light the whole house when powered by your partner's furious pedalling
An old takeaway that can be reheated if you can't be bothered to go to the shops	Tinned food in case of emergencies	A book entitled *The Absolute Idiot's Guide to Cannibalism*

SCIENTIFIC FACTS

The oldest person to have lived reached the age of 122, which means you could not even be halfway there – oh no, another 62 years of *The X Factor*!

· · · · · · · · · ·

The fact that you are 60 is only a state of mind – anything else would be a bit too tiring these days

· · · · · · · · · ·

If it's true that your cells are renewed every seven years, your body is currently just four years old!

HOW TO SURVIVE

When you tell people you have got the latest tablet it's probably not going to be a reference to your iPad

FIRST-DAY DISASTERS

Trying too hard to put a spring in your step
and ending up with your foot in plaster

· · · · · · · · · ·

You go shopping for some fashionable
clothes and find that the buttons on these
modern tops are simply too far apart

· · · · · · · · · ·

You try cultivating a twinkle in your
eye and your partner thinks you
need to see an optometrist

· · · · · · · · · ·

You decide to start sharing the
benefits of your experience but find
everyone prefers Wikipedia

FANTASIES YOU MAY START HAVING

Younger members of the opposite sex
find 60-somethings irresistibly alluring

. . . .

You have been playing the lottery
for so long that statistically you
are bound to win any day now

. . . .

You will one day start to grow a brand
new set of lovely white teeth

The Rover 200 you have
been watching turn to
rust for the past 20 years
is suddenly considered
a classic model

GOOD ROLE MODELS FOR 60-YEAR-OLDS

Any ageing person who others regularly ask: 'What's your secret?'

. . . .

People who think retirement is for wimps

. . . .

People who have to be asked for ID when trying to get a cheaper cinema ticket

ANYONE WHO CAN
GET THROUGH
A WHOLE WEEK
WITHOUT USING
AN ANCIENT
TV COMEDY
CATCHPHRASE FROM
THEIR YOUTH

MEASURES OF SUCCESS

BASIC	ADVANCED
Reaching 60 with your original hips, knees and other major body parts	Actually using them to do anything remotely energetic
Managing to stay ungrumpy most of the time	Still managing to be ungrumpy in the face of cold callers, telephone 'hold' music and automated till voices
You have established a beautiful home for your family	You still live with them in it
You can now appreciate the finer things in life	Your eyesight is still good enough to see things even if they are quite fine

THE WORST THINGS THAT WILL HAPPEN AND HOW TO LOOK AT THEM POSITIVELY

You will find your youthful appearance
can only be maintained in half-
light – which is a fantastic excuse
to rediscover all-night clubbing

. . . .

You realise you are now older than
two-thirds of the entire population
– you will now be able to play the
age card at every opportunity

. . . .

Your memory starts to decline – but this
provides a handy excuse for failing to
attend any appointments you don't fancy

HOW TO SURVIVE

You start to fall over every now and then – but you can learn to incorporate this into an acrobatic routine, pass it off as street performance and collect money from passers-by whenever it happens

MOMENTS WHEN YOU MAY HAVE TO TRY TO CONTROL YOUR TEMPER

When people keep reminding you
that you're 'almost a pensioner'

. . . .

When staff in computer shops assume you
know nothing at all about computers

. . . .

When people in shops keep
asking you if you can manage

. . . .

When complete strangers think it's OK to
refer to you as 'grandad' or 'grandma'

THINGS 60-YEAR-OLDS PROBABLY SHOULDN'T STILL BE DOING

Watching E4, or any other channel that is considered to be for 'the youth'

. . . .

Waking up with no recollection of what you did the night before (well, not due to alcohol anyway)

. . . .

Threatening those who have displeased you with the words 'I bet my dad could fight your dad'

HoW To SURVIVE

Playing computer games
and getting competitive
with teenage relatives

BAD ROLE MODELS FOR 60-YEAR-OLDS

Any ageing person who is regularly threatened by journalists who have 'found out their secret'

. . . .

Any fellow 60-year-old, who people are amazed has reached 60 at all

. . . .

People who have to be asked for ID when mistakenly told to retake their driving test

. . . .

People whose entire range of humorous repartee consists of the catchphrases of people who are no longer alive

IRRITATING THINGS OTHER PEOPLE WILL START DOING TO YOU

Offering you their seats on buses – which is especially awkward when they look your age

. . . .

Pointing out that you are beginning to get a bit shorter and demonstrating this by scoring marks on the kitchen doorframe

. . . .

Casually asking if you have made a will yet

Speaking in an exaggeratedly loud voice when you don't hear something the first time – and quite often the words will be 'It's your round'

WANTED AND UNWANTED NEW FRIENDS

WANTED	UNWANTED
Active 60-year-olds who encourage you to keep fit	60-year-old fitness fanatics who get you up at 6 a.m. for a 10 km run
People who compliment you on how well you're looking	People who compliment you on how well you're looking but add 'for your age' at the end
Young people thrilled to meet a living witness of historic events	People excited to meet a living fossil
Lively energetic people who encourage you to get out of the house	Bailiffs

THINGS THAT WILL BEGIN TO DISTRACT YOU NOW YOU'RE 60

Trying to work out which things
you can now get a discount on

. . . .

Trying to determine which of your
friends has sneakily reached 60
before you without owning up

. . . .

Trying to remember whether it's your
keys or your glasses that you're currently
wandering around the house trying to find

Trying to work out whether the funny noises you can hear are coming from your central heating system or from your own digestive system

THINGS TO KEEP TELLING YOURSELF

Life begins at 60 – if you say it often
enough you may even start to believe it

. . . .

The only reason I have all these lines is
because I spent so much time laughing

. . . .

Life is what you make it – and you know how
everyone makes a mess of DIY projects

SIXTY IS NOT AS
OLD AS IT WAS
WHEN YOU WERE
YOUNG THANKS
TO ADVANCES IN
NUTRITION, MEDICINE
AND PRESERVATIVES

HOW TO PROVE THERE'S PLENTY OF LIFE IN YOU YET

Dust off your glad rags, not your slippers

. . . .

Have a good laugh now and then, though perhaps not while walking along the street on your own

. . . .

Jump up and jog around – and not just when you need the loo

. . . .

Keep up with youth culture rather than constantly shouting 'Ya get me?' at kids you see on the street

DANGERS YOU MAY FACE WHEN CELEBRATING YOUR 60TH BIRTHDAY

Suffering a mild heart attack when your family and friends leap out from behind the sofa shouting 'Surprise!'

. . . .

Dislocation of all the bones in your body when your friends try and give you the bumps (as indeed may happen to all the bones in their bodies in the process)

. . . .

Your false teeth flying out when you try to blow out the candles on your cake

HOW TO SURVIVE

Trying to have a drink for every year of your life

EMOTIONAL RESPONSES YOU SHOULD PRACTISE AS A 60-YEAR-OLD

Event	Appropriate response	Inappropriate response
Somebody makes a disparaging remark about your great age	Grin and remind them that they'll be next	Immediately book appointments for facelifts, teeth whitening and hair transplants
You are asked to take early retirement	Punch the air and rejoice that you will have a few more years of leisure to enjoy	Demand that your boss tells you exactly what they find more attractive about a young fit person on half your salary
You discover your endowment mortgage will not be sufficient to pay off the loan on your house	You meet with your financial adviser to discuss your options	You bulldoze part of your house until you have reduced your property's worth to the same level as your endowment fund
You manage to remove the top from a particularly tight jam jar	You enjoy a moment of quiet satisfaction	You notify all your friends on social media

WAYS IN WHICH YOUR PETS MAY NOW BECOME A DANGER TO YOUR HEALTH

Your dodgy eyesight may result in you tucking into a tin of dog food for your dinner

. . . .

You might do yourself a mischief trying to prise your pampered overweight cat off your lap

. . . .

You will find your pet canary is not a suitable means to identify problems with your gas central heating – invest in a proper carbon monoxide detector instead

Persistently trying to
'change the channel' on your
tropical fish aquarium may
cause you some distress

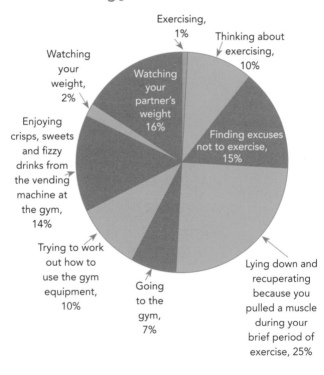

PERCENTAGE OF TIME SPENT ON DIETING AND EXERCISE BY 60-YEAR-OLDS

Exercising, 1%

Thinking about exercising, 10%

Watching your weight, 2%

Watching your partner's weight 16%

Enjoying crisps, sweets and fizzy drinks from the vending machine at the gym, 14%

Finding excuses not to exercise, 15%

Trying to work out how to use the gym equipment, 10%

Going to the gym, 7%

Lying down and recuperating because you pulled a muscle during your brief period of exercise, 25%

SURVIVAL EQUIPMENT THAT 60-YEAR-OLDS SHOULD INVEST IN

A special valve that lets down the 'spare tyre' around your middle

. . . .

A gold credit card wallet to hide your bus pass in

. . . .

Earmuffs that will both keep you warm and prevent you hearing the phone ringing yet again with someone wanting to talk to you about PPI

HOW TO SURVIVE

Virtual-reality goggles that make everything look like it would have done 40 years ago

THINGS YOU USED TO BE ABLE TO DO THAT MAY NOW SEEM DIFFICULT

THING THAT IS BECOMING DIFFICULT TO DO	SUITABLE EXCUSE
Following a conversation in a noisy pub	Why waste valuable drinking time?
Reading bus numbers in the distance	They've made them smaller to comply with government regulations
Getting up from a chair in one continuous movement	Chairs are bigger than they used to be so getting out of them can only be done in stages
Remembering people's names	The world's population is much greater than when you were young so no wonder it's difficult to keep track of everyone

THINGS YOU PROBABLY SHOULDN'T STILL BE DOING AT 60

Going on Club 18–30 holidays

. . . .

Wondering what you're going
to do when you grow up

. . . .

Taking out a substantial 50-year loan

HOW TO SURVIVE

Representing your country at weightlifting, kick-boxing, 100-metre hurdles – basically anything – at the Olympic Games

WHAT BEING 60 DOESN'T HAVE TO MEAN

Slippers and cocoa – instead of a silk slip and spritz of Coco Chanel

. . . .

Dressing gown and a rocking chair – instead of dressing up and a rock concert

. . . .

Giving up – although you can give up getting up early in the morning and not staying out late at night maybe

RETIREMENT — AT
THIS STAGE, YOU
NEED EXCUSES TO
DO MORE, NOT LESS

LESS IMPORTANT AND MORE IMPORTANT THINGS YOU MAY START WORRYING ABOUT

LESS IMPORTANT TO WORRY ABOUT	MORE IMPORTANT TO WORRY ABOUT
A little bit of flab around your middle	A whole lot of flab evenly distributed around your entire body
People teasing you about your age	People taking bets on how much longer you can last
The opposite sex no longer being so interested in you	Medical specialists suddenly taking a great interest in you
Your knees making a cracking sound as you bend them	Your knees making a cracking sound and then bending in the wrong direction

WISHES YOU MIGHT ASK OF A GENIE

To look like a 20-year-old – but maybe
go easy on the tattoos and piercings

. . . .

To have the wisdom of a 60-year-old
but the looks of an 18-year-old
– not the other way round!

. . . .

To have everyone you meet treat you with
enormous care and respect – and not
because they regard you as an ancient relic

HOW TO SURVIVE

To have everything you
touch turn to gold –
or failing that, bonus
shopping saver points,
which may be more likely
thanks to developments
in supermarket
marketing strategies

THE 60-YEAR-OLD'S DAILY INTAKE OF CALORIES FROM A STRICT LOW-FAT DIET

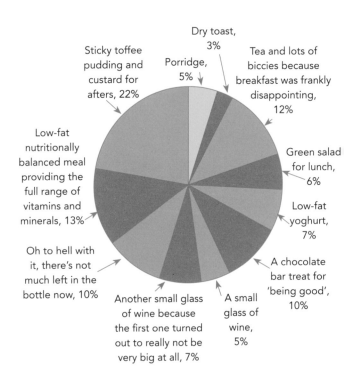

Dry toast, 3%

Porridge, 5%

Tea and lots of biccies because breakfast was frankly disappointing, 12%

Sticky toffee pudding and custard for afters, 22%

Green salad for lunch, 6%

Low-fat nutritionally balanced meal providing the full range of vitamins and minerals, 13%

Low-fat yoghurt, 7%

Oh to hell with it, there's not much left in the bottle now, 10%

A chocolate bar treat for 'being good', 10%

Another small glass of wine because the first one turned out to really not be very big at all, 7%

A small glass of wine, 5%

WHAT WILL YOU BE DOING IN 10 YEARS' TIME

Calling 60-year-olds 'young man' or 'young lady'

• • • • • • • • • •

Clinging on to the notion that you're only just out of your sixties

• • • • • • • • • •

Looking at 60-year-olds you fancy and thinking, 'Cor! If I was just 10 years younger…'

HOW TO SURVIVE

Everything you do now,
but a little more carefully
in case any part of you has
suddenly become even
more delicate following
your seventieth birthday

You prefer using phones
that have buttons

. . . .

You prefer reading books that
don't have buttons

. . . .

You use an alarm clock instead of a
mobile phone to wake you up

. . . .

You take photos on some antiquated
device called a 'camera'

THINK POSITIVELY!

Imagine how terrible it would be to be young now and to be personally preserving all your most embarrassing moments for all time on social media

. . . .

You can now spend many happy hours looking at young people's embarrassing moments on social media

. . . .

In golfing terms, 60 is a very good score and the drinks should probably be on you

In some cultures you'd
be far too young to
be a tribal elder

SELF-HELP BOOKS YOU MIGHT WANT TO READ

Reality Checks for Self-Delusional Sexagenarians

. . . .

How to Cope with Your Income Being Slashed on Retirement

. . . .

Why There Is Nothing Wrong With Your Eyesight (large print edition)

. . . .

The Seven Signs of Ageing – How to Claim Your Prize When You Collect the Set

Why don't they have Club 18–60 holidays?

. . . .

My best-before date has
now probably passed

. . . .

When I start claiming my pension, will
there be any chance of promotion or
any sort of productivity bonus?

. . . .

Have I left it too late to embark on a
life of depravity and debauchery?

HOW TO MAINTAIN ENTHUSIASM

Keep your chin up, and if that doesn't
work, keep them both up

. . . .

Tell yourself that you will never be more
than '60-something' for the next decade

. . . .

If life begins at 40, that must mean
you only recently left school

KEEP SMILING —
EVEN IF IT'S ONLY
BECAUSE THEY
MADE YOUR NEW
DENTURES A BIT
TOO BIG

If you're interested in finding out more about our books, find us on Facebook at Summersdale Publishers and follow us on Twitter at @Summersdale.

www.summersdale.com